S0-EAV-714

WITHDRAWN

# Walter Cronkite

## The Most Trusted Man In America

### by Paul Westman

### Illustrated by Reg Sandland

DILLON PRESS, INC. MINNEAPOLIS, MINNESOTA

Library of Congress Cataloging in Publication Data

Westman, Paul
   Walter Cronkite: the most trusted man in America.

   (Taking Part; 6)
   SUMMARY: A brief biography of the CBS newsman,
anchorman for television's longest-running news
show.
   1. Cronkite, Walter—Juvenile literature.
   2. Journalists—United States—Biography—Juvenile
literature.
   [1. Cronkite, Walter. 2. Journalists] I. Sandland, Reg. II.
Title.
   PN4874.C84W4     070.4'092'4 [B] [92]      79-22686

   ISBN 0-87518-187-2

©1980 by Dillon Press, Inc. All rights reserved

Second printing 1981

Dillon Press, Inc., 500 South Third Street
Minneapolis, Minnesota 55415

Printed in the United States of America

# WALTER CRONKITE

Walter Cronkite is invited daily into the home of millions of Americans. When he says, "And that's the way it is," at the end of the "CBS Evening News," people believe him. In fact, public opinion polls have shown Cronkite to be the most trusted person in America. His news show has become the standard by which all other TV news shows are measured.

During more than forty years in the news business, Walter Cronkite has covered a lot of big stories. He has criss-crossed the globe many times. Space flights, peace missions, moon landings, summit meetings, elections, funerals, wars, and floods have all been part of his beat.

Walter Cronkite liked growing up in Kansas City, Missouri, in 1924. In Kansas City there were plenty of things for a boy to do. Walter and his friends played games together—football, baseball, tag, and marbles. They flew kites on the flat, windy Missouri prairie. They went fishing and swimming, too.

Sometimes the boys got into fights. But Walter never did. He was not a scrapper. If a fight started, Walter tried to talk the two boys into being friends.

Walter Leland Cronkite, Jr., was born on November 4, 1916, in St. Joseph, Missouri. St. Joseph is on the Missouri River not far from Kansas City. Once St. Joseph had been the gateway to the wild west. From there the Pony Express riders had carried the mail to California.

Walter had no brothers or sisters. Even though

he was an only child, he had lots of friends. He was an easygoing and likeable boy.

When Walter was still small, the Cronkites moved to Kansas City. There Dr. Cronkite, a dentist, opened a new practice. Walter's mother, Helen, tended the house. Often Walter helped her with such chores as beating rugs, cleaning, or washing dishes.

The Cronkites lived in a nice house in a nice neighborhood. Walter's father had a good job and was his own boss. But the Cronkites were by no means rich. They were just like many other American families of the 1920s.

When Walter was growing up, many of his relatives came to visit. Aunts, uncles, cousins, and grandparents lived nearby.

One of Walter's aunts studied the family tree. Walter found out that among his ancestors was a group of Dutch merchants. These merchants had come to America from Holland. They had settled in New York City in the 1600s. At that time the city was called New Amsterdam because so many Dutch lived there. The Cronkites had not come west until Grandpa Cronkite moved to Missouri.

But Walter's favorite person was his Grandpa Fritsche. Grandpa Fritsche was a druggist. He was a tall man, with a shock of gray hair and great shaggy eyebrows. He owned a pharmacy in Fort Leavenworth, Kansas.

The pharmacy was a wonderful place. Dozens of

glass bottles lined the shelves. They were marked with Latin names and filled with powders and liquids. There was a marble counter with metal stools where people could order sodas and ice cream. The store had a nice smell all its own.

One night Grandpa's pharmacy caught fire. Everyone in the family hurried downtown. Great clouds of smoke rose into the sky from the fierce blaze. Firemen rushed to and fro with ladders and fire hoses. But there was nothing they could do. The store burned to the ground.

After the fire Grandpa Fritsche opened a new drugstore in Kansas City. Business was so good that he had to hire two clerks to help him run it.

Many people who came to the store had little money. Soon they owed large bills. Finally Grandpa hired Walter to collect the bills.

Walter visited all the people who owed his grandfather money. Some lived in run-down houses. Others had patches on their clothes. None of them had any money to give him.

Grandpa listened as Walter told him how poor the people were. Then he took out his big account book. Behind each name he wrote the words "Paid in full." Walter never forgot his grandfather's kindness.

When Walter was 10, the Cronkites moved again.

This time they went to Houston, Texas. Dr. Cronkite became a teacher at the University of Texas Dental School in Houston.

Houston was an oil town. It was a busy, noisy place. Trucks rumbled through the streets. Ships entered and left the harbor. It was a big change from the prairie town of Kansas City.

Soon Walter turned his thoughts toward work.
What should he be when he grew up? He wanted a
job full of adventure, one that would let him see the
world. He thought of becoming a mining engineer.
But in school he was not very good at math and
science.

Then one day Walter read a short story in *American Boy* magazine. The story told about the adventures of a reporter, or journalist. Reporters, Walter learned, traveled to exciting places. They wrote about shipwrecks, fires, and even battles. Their stories appeared in newspapers around the country. This was the job for Walter Cronkite!

At San Jacinto High School, Walter had a chance to begin his career as a journalist. He worked as a reporter for the school paper, the *Campus Cub*. It was an exciting moment when he first saw his name in print. Walter also wrote for the school yearbook.

In 1933 Walter entered the University of Texas. He took courses in politics, economics, and journalism. These were the subjects he liked best.

The 1930s were the years of the Great Depression. Thousands of people lost their jobs. Many went hungry.

Walter needed money to help pay his college expenses. He was luckier than many because he had a job. In fact, he had three jobs.

One of Walter's jobs was to report campus news for the *Houston Post*. He wrote stories for the paper about what happened at the university. On another job Walter covered politics at the Texas state capitol. These stories were used by the Scripps-Howard newspaper chain. His third job was as a sportscaster for a Houston radio station.

With so much work to do, Walter began skipping

classes. He spent more and more time covering politics at the capitol. For Walter this was much more exciting than school. Finally he dropped out of college.

Walter became a full-time reporter for the *Hous-*

*ton Post.* He wrote articles on any subject he was given to cover, from church services to news stories.

In 1937 Walter moved back to Kansas City. There he took a job as a sportscaster at radio station KCMO. In those days many small stations could not afford to broadcast games live. Instead, they would send just one reporter to watch the game. The reporter would send back telegrams describing what was happening.

When Cronkite received the telegrams, he was expected to fake the game on the air. He did so by calling out the plays as if they were happening before his eyes. He also played recordings of college fight songs and cheering crowds. Many listeners thought he was really at the game.

In Kansas City Walter met a young woman named Mary Elizabeth Maxwell. Everyone called her Betsy. Betsy was a reporter, too. She wrote a newspaper column for the *Kansas City Journal.* Walter and Betsy decided to get married. In 1940, when Walter's pay was raised to $35 a week, they did.

A year earlier Cronkite had left his radio job to work as a writer for United Press, or UP. UP was a wire service. Its reporters were stationed all over the world. The reporters wrote news stories about major events in their part of the world. Then United Press sent the stories by teletype to newspapers.

Cronkite liked working as a United Press reporter. He even enjoyed the tiresome tasks that most reporters shunned. Reporting, editing, deadlines, and even the smell of the newsroom appealed to him.

For two years Cronkite worked as a UP reporter in the Midwest. Then, in December 1941, the United States entered World War II. UP sent Cronkite to Europe to cover the war.

Being a war correspondent was risky. But it was

exciting, too. When U.S. troops landed in North Africa, Walter Cronkite was with them. He wrote about the Battle of the North Atlantic. He flew on Allied bombers over Europe. When German planes attacked his squadron, he even manned a big machine gun. Once a German buzz bomb struck his London apartment.

In 1944 Cronkite covered the important D-Day invasion of France. He parachuted into Holland with Allied troops. Later he crash-landed in a glider at the Battle of Arnhem.

Before long the Germans were in retreat across Europe. By this time Cronkite was a highly respected reporter. He was given the job of setting up UP news bureaus in the newly-freed countries of Belgium, Holland, and Luxembourg.

Sometimes Cronkite was the first outsider to arrive in these countries. People thought he was a general or government official. They cheered him, threw flowers in his path, and honored him with speeches. He was treated like a conquering hero. Later the real troops arrived. They were not pleased to learn that a reporter had stolen their glory.

After the war UP picked Cronkite to be their chief reporter at the Nuremberg trials. These were war crimes trials held in the German city of Nuremberg. There, many high-ranking Nazis were brought to justice.

Cronkite's next beat, or news assignment, was

Moscow, the capital of Russia. During World War II, Russia had fought with the Allies against Germany. Now that the war was over, things had changed. Russia was a communist country. It had used its power to take over many of the countries in Eastern Europe. There were bad feelings between the Allies and the Russians.

Cronkite did not like Russia. Reporters there were closely watched by the secret police. They could not travel freely or talk to the people. And they could print only what the Russian government allowed them to print.

In 1948 Cronkite was glad to leave Moscow. But now he had another worry. There was a baby, Nancy, to support. Soon Walter and Betsy had two more children—Kathy and Walter Cronkite III, nicknamed "Chip." Walter found that he could not support a growing family on a reporter's small salary.

The pay in radio was much better. Once more Cronkite returned to radio reporting. This time he covered the nation's capital, Washington, D.C. His broadcasts were heard by listeners in Kansas, Missouri, and Nebraska.

At this time a new invention was coming into American homes. It was called television. By 1949 thousands of people owned TV sets. More and more shows were being shown.

Walter Cronkite was one of the first journalists to work for a TV network. In 1950 he went to work for CBS News.

That year the Korean War broke out. Cronkite wanted to go to Korea to cover the fighting. Instead, he was given the job of explaining the war's progress to TV viewers. Using maps and a blackboard, he explained each day's fighting.

Cronkite was so good at this job that CBS chose him to cover the 1952 presidential conventions. Two conventions were held, one by the Democrats and one by the Republicans.

At the conventions each party chose a candidate to run for president. In 1952 the Democrats chose Adlai Stevenson. The Republicans chose General Dwight D. Eisenhower. These were the first two conventions to receive full TV coverage.

Before he went on the air, Cronkite learned

everything he could about the convention process.
He learned about the politicians who would be there,
too. His live reports were so clear, fact-filled, and
lively that they made him famous.

During the 1950s Cronkite was a roving reporter
for CBS. He had many different assignments. Sometimes he hosted in-depth news programs dealing
with one subject. At other times he hosted entertain-
ment shows. He traveled around the world covering
major stories.

One of his most popular shows was "You Are There." "You Are There" was a weekly series which re-created famous events from history. Each Sunday Cronkite had his own newscast, the "Sunday News Special."

By this time Cronkite was making a great deal of money. He was famous. Now he had the chance to try some of the things he had always wanted to do.

One thing Walter wanted to try was sailing. He bought a 35-foot boat called the *Wyntie*. On weekends and holidays the Cronkites went sailing. Later, when the *Wyntie* became too old, Walter bought a new boat, the *Wyntje*. It was named for one of his Dutch ancestors. The Cronkites sailed the *Wyntje* everywhere from Massachusetts to the Caribbean.

Another thing Walter wanted to try was sports car racing. He took part in many races. In one he was almost killed.

Walter was driving a Triumph TR-3 in a road race. The race was held in the Great Smoky Mountains of Tennessee. Suddenly his car plunged off the side of the road at high speed. It rolled end over end down a hill, and landed in a lake. Luckily, Walter climbed out unhurt.

At CBS one of Cronkite's important jobs was covering the American space program. Starting in 1956, he headed all CBS space coverage.

Cronkite liked this job more than any other. He read everything he could find about rockets and space. Once he flew in a special plane to find out what it was like to be weightless. He felt the great pressures an astronaut feels during liftoff. Soon he was an expert on space.

In 1961 Alan Shepard became the first American in space. Many TV viewers listened to Cronkite describe Shepard's historic 15-minute flight.

The next year John Glenn became the first American to orbit, or circle, the earth. Cronkite covered this history-making space flight, too.

But the biggest space story of all was the *Apollo 11* moon landing. On this mission Neil Armstrong became the first human to set foot on the moon. To cover the story for CBS, Cronkite was on the air for 18 hours straight. After a six-hour nap, he was on the air again for nine more hours.

Cronkite made the space flights easy for viewers

*Astronaut Edwin Aldrin walked on the moon with Neil Armstrong. Armstrong can be seen in the reflection from Aldrin's sun visor.*

to understand. No matter what the subject—wars, political conventions, or peace missions—he could explain it clearly and simply. Many thought he was one of the best newscasters of his time.

On April 16, 1962, Walter Cronkite took over the job of anchoring the "CBS Evening News." This meant that each night he reported the news to millions of TV viewers. He also helped write and arrange it. His show was called "The CBS Evening News with Walter Cronkite."

In those days network news shows were only 15 minutes long. Network officials thought viewers would turn off a longer news show. Most people, they felt, didn't like to watch the news.

But in September 1963, CBS decided to change its news show. That month Walter Cronkite broadcast the first daily 30-minute TV news program. For it he interviewed President John F. Kennedy at Kennedy's home in Cape Cod, Massachusetts. It didn't take long for ABC and NBC to switch to the 30-minute news show, too.

One day Cronkite was taking a break at his desk.

*Walter Cronkite interviews President John F. Kennedy.*

It was Friday, November 22, 1963. The newsroom was quiet. Most of the crew was out to lunch. Cronkite relaxed. He put his feet on his desk and opened a newspaper.

A wild-eyed man rushed into the newsroom. "President Kennedy's just been shot!" he gasped.

Cronkite leaped to his feet and dashed to a teletype machine. He tore off the latest copy. Then he went on the air to break the tragic news to the nation in a special bulletin.

At first the news wires were crowded. Confusion made it hard to know what had really happened. But soon the facts could be pieced together. President John F. Kennedy had been killed by a gunman in Dallas, Texas during a parade.

When Cronkite announced the president's death, his voice cracked and his eyes filled with tears. It was the only time Walter Cronkite ever broke down on

camera. He had even forgotten to put on his suit coat. He announced the president's death in his shirt-sleeves.

President Kennedy's death stunned the nation. That same day all three TV networks stopped their regular programs. For four days only news stories about the president's death and funeral were shown. Through television millions of Americans shared their feelings of sadness and loss.

Later in the 1960s, other well-known people were killed. In 1968 Robert Kennedy, the president's brother, and Martin Luther King, Jr., the black civil rights leader, were shot. Cronkite covered these stories, too.

Before the 1960s TV news was not as important as print news. Cameras, sound machines, and rolls of film were bulky. It took a great deal of time to get film reports back to the studio. By that time newspapers and magazines had already printed the news story.

But two inventions made TV news reporting a lot faster. One was the satellite. The other was videotape. Videotape was much easier to handle than rolls of film. It greatly speeded up the time needed to make TV news reports. And by satellite, pictures and sound could be relayed around the world instantly. People stopped relying on newspapers as their main source of news. They turned to television instead. And, more and more, they tuned in Walter Cronkite.

"The CBS Evening News" was shown at 6:30 each weeknight. Before the show started, Cronkite worked on the script he was to read. He went through it slowly, timing himself with a stopwatch. Sometimes he crossed out words with a blue pencil.

Five minutes before air time, the countdown began. At three minutes Cronkite was still busy reading and making changes. At two minutes he was combing his hair and putting on his suit coat. Then he faced the camera.

Cronkite ended each show with the words, "And that's the way it is. This is Walter Cronkite, CBS News, good night." These words became well known to millions of American families.

*Cronkite ended each "CBS Evening News" show with the words, "And that's the way it is."*

The 1960s were an exciting time to be a reporter. Civil rights marches, riots, protests, and space shots made headlines across the nation. Major news stories seemed to break almost every day.

One of the biggest news stories was the Vietnam War. The Vietnam War split the nation in two. Many Americans believed strongly that the war was wrong. Thousands of young men refused to serve in the army when they were drafted. People showed their anger through protest marches and riots.

In 1965 Cronkite visited Vietnam, a small country in Southeast Asia. American troops were fighting Vietnamese communist troops there. At this time the war was still small. The protests in the United States had just begun. Cronkite approved of what he saw in Vietnam. He thought the United States was doing the right thing.

In 1968 he returned to Vietnam. This time he spoke to hundreds of officials and military men. He visited towns and villages. In the town of Hue, he watched Americans fighting in the streets.

Things had changed a great deal since 1965. The

*Cronkite traveled to Vietnam to learn firsthand about the war.*

war was much larger. Cronkite came to believe that American troops would not win the war. He thought that we were doing more harm than good.

As the fighting dragged on, the Vietnamese people suffered greatly. Many of their villages were destroyed. Much of their farmland could not produce crops. And more and more of their people were killed—women and children as well as soldiers.

On TV Cronkite said that the United States should make peace with the Vietnamese.

"We lived up to our pledge to defend democracy," he said, "and we did the best we could." This was the first time Cronkite had expressed an opinion on the air. His words were calm and thoughtful.

Many journalists had strong views on subjects like Vietnam. If they wanted to, they could choose facts to suit their own views. "Coloring" the news gave them power. And some journalists used this power.

Walter Cronkite did not believe in coloring facts. He believed in the truth. Given the truth, people could make up their own minds.

This sense of fairness helped make Cronkite the most-watched newscaster in America. In fact, one poll showed that he was the most trusted person in the country. People trusted Walter Cronkite more than they did the president of the United States.

In the early 1970s, some government leaders thought TV newscasters had too much power. The best known of these leaders was Vice-President Agnew. He wanted to place limits on the kind of news that could be reported.

These leaders made Cronkite angry. He believed in freedom of the press. Such freedom was granted by the Constitution. For nearly two hundred years, it had been the right of all U.S. citizens. No government official should be able to take it away.

Cronkite was respected. He knew that people listened to what he had to say. Now, he decided, it was time for him to speak out. He made speeches. And he defended freedom of the press before Congress.

"A threat against one newsman is an attack against us all," Cronkite warned. "We use the peo-

ple's air, but this does not mean that the government can say what goes over it."

Because Cronkite spoke out, some government leaders attacked his views. But these attacks didn't scare Walter. He kept on saying what he thought was right.

Later some of these same leaders were part of the Watergate affair. This was the biggest news story of the 1970s. And Cronkite played a big part in it.

Watergate was the name of a building in Washington, D.C. During the 1972 election campaign, the Democratic Party had its offices there. Late one night a group of men broke into the offices. The burglars were caught. They had been hired to steal information that might hurt the Democrats.

Reporters were slow to report the Watergate affair. Newspapers were quicker than TV. But four months after the break-in, Cronkite gave two long reports on the "CBS Evening News." For the first time, millions of people learned the full story of the break-in. Cronkite's courage helped make Watergate a household word.

Later it was learned that men close to President Richard Nixon had helped plan the break-in. Nixon himself had tried to cover it up. In 1974 Congress took the first steps to remove him from office. He resigned instead. He was the first president ever to do so.

*Walter Cronkite was the host of a radio talk show with President Jimmy Carter.*

In 1976 Jimmy Carter became president. Carter tried to bring government closer to the people. One thing he did was to hold a radio talk show. Anyone who wanted could phone the president and talk to him.

Walter Cronkite was part of this historic broadcast. Many people phoned to express their problems and hopes to the president. They were pleased to be able to speak to him in person.

"Walter, I liked it," President Carter said when the show was over. "I'd like to do it again sometime."

One of President Carter's biggest worries was the Middle East. The Arabs and the Israelis did not get along there. Since 1948 they had gone to war four times. The president was afraid that a major war could break out at any time.

The two main foes in the Middle East were Israel and Egypt. Israel's leader was Menachem Begin. Anwar Sadat was the leader of Egypt.

President Carter wanted to bring these two men together. He wanted to help bring peace to the Middle East. But no Arab leader had ever gone to Israel. And no Israeli leader had ever gone to Egypt.

In 1977 Walter Cronkite interviewed Anwar Sadat. Cronkite knew that both Begin and Sadat wanted peace. He asked Sadat, "What are your terms for talking with Mr. Begin?"

Sadat listed all the things Israel would have to do. Cronkite had expected this reply. But he wanted to make sure that he had the story straight. He asked the question once more.

*Cronkite has interviewed many world leaders. One of them was Egypt's leader, Anwar Sadat.*

"So those are your terms before you'll even speak with Mr. Begin?" Cronkite asked.

"No! No! No!" Sadat answered. "Those are my terms for peace."

"You mean you'd visit Israel without those terms?"

"Of course."

Cronkite knew he had a big story. "When?" he asked.

"Whenever Mr. Begin invites me," Sadat replied.

"This week?" Cronkite asked.

"Yes, if he'll have me."

Cronkite rushed to a phone. He called Prime Minister Begin and told him what Sadat had said. Begin was surprised, but pleased. "I'll have him this week," he told Cronkite.

On the "CBS Evening News," Cronkite spoke with both leaders again. Begin was in Israel. Sadat was in Egypt. A satellite broadcast brought them face-to-face.

Begin invited Sadat to come to Israel. Sadat said he would come. It was an important moment for world peace.

Sadat did visit Israel. He was welcomed by cheering crowds. Two old foes had come together at last. Later, President Carter invited both leaders to Camp David. At Camp David they signed a peace treaty.

Many reporters had tried to find the "inside story" about the Middle East. Peter Jennings of ABC had just missed getting this story before Cronkite. Jennings sent a message to his rival. "I wish you'd retire," he said. "Congratulations again."

During more than 40 years in the news business, Walter Cronkite has covered a lot of big stories. He has criss-crossed the globe many times. Space flights, peace missions, moon landings, summit meetings, elections, funerals, wars, and floods have all been part of his beat.

As Cronkite would say, "And that's the way it is."

## The Author

Paul Westman is a regular contributor to *Current Biography* and has written many books for young people, including several for the Taking Part series. Of the series, Westman says, "Young readers will learn something about well-known contemporary men and women in many challenging fields and at the same time begin to discover some of the joys of reading."

A recent graduate of the University of Minnesota, Westman lives in Minneapolis.

## The Illustrator

Reg Sandland is a freelance illustrator and graphic designer whose work has appeared in numerous newspapers and magazines, as well as one previous book. He is a graduate of Bemidji State University and has attended the University of Minnesota and the Minneapolis College of Art and Design.

*Photographs are reproduced through the courtesy of CBS News and the National Aeronautics and Space Administration.*

## DATE DUE

| NOV 27 1995 | | | |
|---|---|---|---|
| | | | |
| | | | |
| | | | |
| | | | |
| | | | |
| | | | |
| | | | |
| | | | |
| | | | |
| | | | |
| | | | |
| | | | |
| | | | |
| | | | |

HIGHSMITH 45-102        PRINTED IN U.S.A.